The Therapeutic Power of the Vagus Nerve

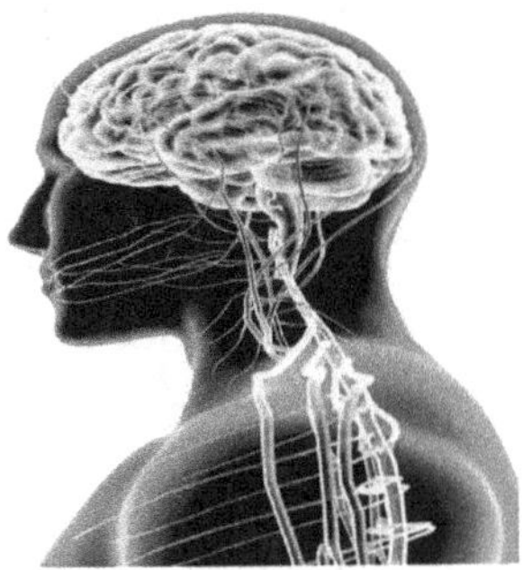

Understanding How to Control Inflammation, Calm Anxiety, Stimulate and Activate your Immune System and Overcome Depression

John C. Nail

Table of Contents

Introduction..**5**

What are the advantages of activating the vagus nerve?..7

Chapter 1: Anatomy and Physiology of the Vagus Nerve....................................... **10**

The Origin and Branches of the Vagus Nerve.10

The Vagus Nerve Functions and Roles in many Organs and Systems.......................................14

Vagus Nerve and Autonomic Nervous System... 17

Vagus Nerve and Inflammatory Reaction........19

Chapter 2: The Vagus Nerve and Stress...........**23**

How does stress influence the vagus nerve and vice versa?..23

The vagus nerve and the hypothalamic-pituitary-adrenal (HPA) axis......26

The vagus nerve and the cortisol response and The vagus nerve and the immune system......29

Chapter 3: The Vagus Nerve and Mental Health..33

Vagus Nerve and Mental Problems.................33

Vagus Nerve and Anxiety Disorders.............. 34

The Vagus Nerve and PTSD.........................36

Vagus Nerve and Cognitive Functioning.........37

Chapter 4: "The Vagus Nerve and Physical Health".. **39**

Vagus nerve and cardiovascular health.......... 39

Vagus nerve and intestinal health................... 41

Vagus Nerve and Respiratory Health.............45

Vagus nerve and metabolic health..................47

Chapter 5: How to Naturally Stimulate the Vagus Nerve..49

Breathing exercises and strategies.................49

Meditation and mindfulness methods............. 52

Yoga and other physical exercises..................55

Singing, Humming, and Chanting................... 58

Chapter 6: How to Stimulate the Vagus Nerve with Technology...61

Transcutaneous vagus nerve stimulation (tVNS) 61

Auricular vagus nerve stimulation (aVNS)...... 64

Invasive vagus nerve stimulation (iVNS).........67

Biofeedback and neurofeedback devices....... 69

Chapter 7: How to Incorporate Vagus Nerve Stimulation into Your Daily Life........................72

Conclusion.. 82

Introduction

The vagus nerve is a main nerve that links your brain to other organs in your body, including your heart, lungs, stomach, and intestines. It is part of the parasympathetic nervous system, which is in charge of keeping your body calm and functioning normally.

The vagus nerve influences your physical and mental health in a number of ways, including:

- Controlling your heart rate, blood pressure, and respiration. The vagus nerve instructs your heart to slow down or speed up, depending on your demands. It also regulates the muscles in your airways and lungs, allowing you to breathe deeper or shallower. A healthy vagus nerve may reduce your risk of heart disease, stroke, and hypertension.

- Controlling your digestion and metabolism. The vagus nerve increases the creation of saliva, stomach acid, and digestive enzymes, all of which help you digest and absorb food. It also controls the flow of food through your intestines and the secretion of hormones that influence your appetite and blood sugar levels. A healthy vagus nerve can help prevent or treat digestive issues like irritable bowel syndrome, gastroparesis, and obesity.

- Modifying your immune system and inflammation. The vagus nerve detects and responds to infections and injuries in your body by delivering signals to produce chemicals that combat inflammation and promote healing. It also affects the functioning of immune cells like macrophages and lymphocytes, which assist in removing diseases and foreign substances. A healthy vagus nerve can help you avoid chronic inflammatory disorders including rheumatoid arthritis, diabetes, and asthma.

- Influencing your mood and emotions. The vagus nerve connects your brain to your face muscles, vocal cords, and ears, all of which contribute to emotional expression and perception. It also links your brain and stomach, which create neurotransmitters like serotonin and dopamine that influence your mood and behavior. A healthy vagus nerve helps improve your social and emotional abilities, including empathy, compassion, and communication. It can also help you feel less stressed, anxious, and depressed.

As you can see, the vagus nerve plays an important role in your physical and emotional well-being. You may boost the function and advantages of your vagus nerve by stimulating it naturally or with technology. You may learn more about how to activate your vagus nerve in the book outline I sent in the previous mail. I hope you found it useful and interesting.

What are the advantages of activating the vagus nerve?

Stimulating the vagus nerve can have a range of advantages for your physical and mental health, including:

- Enhancing your mood while lowering stress, anxiety, and sadness. The vagus nerve connects your brain and intestines, releasing chemicals that influence your emotions. Stimulating the vagus nerve can boost levels of serotonin and dopamine, which are linked to pleasure and well-being.

- Increasing your cognitive abilities and memory. The vagus nerve also connects the brain to the ears, which are responsible for hearing and language. Stimulating the vagus nerve can boost your auditory processing, language capabilities, and learning capacities.

- Reducing your blood pressure and heart rate. The vagus nerve controls your cardiovascular system by providing messages to the heart and blood vessels. Stimulating the vagus nerve activates the parasympathetic nervous system, which relaxes the body and lowers blood pressure and heart rate.

- Boosting your immune system and reducing inflammation. The vagus nerve detects and responds to infections and injuries in your body by delivering signals to produce chemicals that combat inflammation and promote healing. It also affects the function of immunological cells, which aid in the elimination of diseases and foreign substances.

- Improving your digestion and metabolism. The vagus nerve increases the creation of saliva, stomach acid, and digestive enzymes, all of which help you digest and absorb food. It also controls the flow of food through your intestines and the secretion of hormones that influence your appetite and blood sugar levels.

Chapter 1: Anatomy and Physiology of the Vagus Nerve

The Origin and Branches of the Vagus Nerve

The vagus nerve is the tenth cranial nerve (CN X) and the longest in the body. It emerges from the medulla oblongata of the brain stem and leaves the skull via the jugular foramen. It then passes through the neck, thorax, and belly, releasing different branches along the route. The vagus nerve is a mixed nerve, which means it has sensory and motor fibers. It is most closely related with the autonomic nervous system's parasympathetic division, which governs internal organ functioning. It also transmits sensory information from the skin, mucous membranes, and taste buds.

Origin and branches of the vagus nerve:
- Origin: The vagus nerve is formed from four nuclei in the medulla oblongata: the dorsal nucleus, the nucleus ambiguus, the solitary

nucleus, and the spinal trigeminal nucleus. These nuclei give birth to several kinds of fibers that comprise the vagus nerve. The dorsal nucleus delivers parasympathetic fibers to the intestines. The nucleus ambiguus provides efferent motor and parasympathetic fibers to the heart, as well as pharyngeal, laryngeal, and soft palate muscles. The tongue sends specific gustatory afferent fibers to the solitary nucleus, while the organs send visceral afferent fibers. The skin and mucous membranes of the head and neck send general sensory afferent fibers to the spinal trigeminal nucleus.

- Branching in the jugular fossa: The vagus nerve, together with the glossopharyngeal and accessory nerves (CN IX and XI), leaves the skull via the jugular foramen. The vagus nerve gives birth to two branches in the jugular fossa: the meningeal and auricular branches. The meningeal branch nourishes the dura mater in the posterior cerebral fossa. The auricular branch supplies the skin of the external ear as well as the external auditory canal.

- Neck branches: The carotid sheath contains the vagus nerve, the internal jugular vein, and the common carotid artery. It gives rise to various branches in the neck, including the pharyngeal, superior, and recurrent laryngeal nerves, as well as the superior cardiac branches. The pharyngeal branches connect the glossopharyngeal nerve to the sympathetic trunk, forming the pharyngeal plexus. They innervate the majority of the pharyngeal and soft palate muscles, with the exception of the stylopharyngeus and the tensor veli palatini. The superior laryngeal nerve is separated into the internal and external laryngeal nerves. The internal laryngeal nerve supplies sensory innervation to the laryngopharynx and upper section of the larynx. The external laryngeal nerve innervates the cricothyroid muscle in the larynx. The recurrent laryngeal nerve wraps around the subclavian artery on the right side and the aortic arch on the left side before ascending to the larynx. It innervates the majority of the laryngeal intrinsic muscles, with the exception of the cricothyroid, as well as the inferior section of the larynx. The superior cardiac branches connect with the cardiac plexus and give parasympathetic innervation to the heart.

- Thoracic branches: The vagus nerve enters the thorax and divides into two trunks: anterior and posterior. The posterior vagal trunk is formed by the right vagus nerve and runs behind the esophagus and stomach. The anterior vagal trunk is formed by the left vagus nerve and travels in front of the esophagus and stomach. The vagal trunks give rise to various branches in the thorax, including the inferior cardiac nerve, anterior and posterior bronchial branches, and esophageal branches. The inferior cardiac nerve connects to the cardiac plexus, providing parasympathetic innervation to the heart. The anterior and posterior bronchial branches deliver parasympathetic and sensory fibers to the trachea and bronchi. The esophageal branches create the esophageal plexus, which innervates the esophagus and lower esophageal sphincter[12].

- Abdominal Branches: The vagus nerve enters the abdomen after passing via the diaphragm and esophagus. The anterior and posterior vagal trunks produce multiple branches in the belly, including the gastric, celiac, and hepatic branches. The gastric branches provide the stomach with parasympathetic and sensory fibers. Celiac branches are mostly generated from the right vagus nerve. They connect to the celiac plexus, which innervates the pancreas, kidneys, spleen, suprarenal glands, and intestines. The hepatic branches are mostly derived from the left vagus nerve. They connect to the hepatic plexus, which innervates the liver, gallbladder, and bile ducts.

The Vagus Nerve Functions and Roles in many Organs and Systems.

- **Cardiovascular system:** The vagus nerve controls your heartbeat, blood pressure, and blood vessel dilation. It signals your heart to slow down or speed up, depending on your demands. It also regulates the muscles in your blood vessels, allowing them to contract or relax. A healthy vagus nerve may reduce your risk of heart disease, stroke, and hypertension.
- **Respiratory system:** The vagus nerve regulates respiration and airway constriction. It transmits messages to your lungs and bronchi, adjusting your breathing rate and depth based on your oxygen and carbon dioxide levels. It also regulates the muscles in your airways, allowing them to contract or relax. A healthy vagus nerve can help prevent or treat respiratory conditions like asthma, chronic obstructive pulmonary disease (COPD), and sleep apnea.

- **Digestive system:** The vagus nerve controls your digestion and metabolism. It increases the production of saliva, stomach acid, and digestive enzymes, all of which help you digest and absorb food.

- **Urinary system:** The vagus nerve regulates your urine and bladder function. It delivers signals to your kidneys to regulate pee output, as well as to your bladder, to control muscular contraction and relaxation. A healthy vagus nerve can help prevent or treat urinary problems like incontinence, overactive bladder, and urinary tract infections.

- **Endocrine system**: The vagus nerve controls hormone secretion and regulation. It communicates with your pituitary gland, thyroid gland, adrenal glands, and pancreas to control the release of hormones that influence your development, metabolism, stress response, and blood sugar levels. A healthy vagus nerve can help prevent or treat endocrine problems including hypothyroidism, diabetes, and obesity.

- **Immune system:** The vagus nerve controls the immune system and inflammation. It delivers messages to your spleen, lymph nodes, and bone marrow to control the creation and activity of immune cells including macrophages, lymphocytes, and natural killer cells. It also instructs your brain to release chemicals that combat inflammation and promote healing, such as acetylcholine, norepinephrine, and cytokines. A healthy vagus nerve can help you avoid chronic inflammatory disorders including rheumatoid arthritis, diabetes, and asthma.

- **Nervous system:** The vagus nerve joins your brain and gut, creating the brain-gut axis. It transmits and receives signals between your central nervous system and your enteric nervous system, which regulates the operations of your digestive tract. It also regulates the creation and function of neurotransmitters including serotonin, dopamine, and gamma-aminobutyric acid (GABA), all of which have an impact on your mood, behavior, and cognition. A healthy vagus nerve can improve your mental health and well-being by avoiding or treating mood, anxiety, cognitive, and neurodegenerative illnesses.

Vagus Nerve and Autonomic Nervous System

The vagus nerve is the primary nerve of the autonomic nervous system's parasympathetic division, hence the two are inextricably linked. The autonomic nervous system regulates the body's involuntary activities, including heart rate, blood pressure, respiration, digestion, and metabolism. It is composed of two parts: sympathetic and parasympathetic. The sympathetic system primes the body for action by raising awareness, energy, and blood supply to the muscles. The parasympathetic nervous system relaxes the body by lowering heart rate, blood pressure, and tension.

- - Controlling heart rate and blood pressure by delivering signals to the heart and blood vessels to slow down or speed up in response to the body's demands.
- - Regulating breathing and airway constriction by delivering signals to the lungs and bronchi to modify the pace and depth of breathing, as well as to the airway muscles to constrict or relax.

- - Stimulating digestion and metabolism by sending signals to the stomach, intestines, pancreas, and liver to produce saliva, gastric acid, digestive enzymes, and hormones that aid in the breakdown and absorption of food, as well as regulating food movement through the digestive tract and blood sugar levels.
- - Controlling the immune system and inflammation by sending signals to the spleen, lymph nodes, and bone marrow to control immune cell production and activity, as well as to the brain to release chemicals that combat inflammation and promote healing.
- - Influencing mood and emotions via sending and receiving signals between the brain and the stomach, which generates neurotransmitters that impact mood and behavior, as well as linking the brain to the face muscles, voice cords, and ears, which are involved in emotion expression and perception.

The vagus nerve can be activated naturally or through technology, depending on the individual's requirements and preferences.

Natural ways to stimulate the vagus nerve include breathing exercises, meditation, yoga, singing, and humming. Transcutaneous, auricular, and invasive vagus nerve stimulation devices are three examples of technical ways for stimulating the vagus nerve. Stimulating the vagus nerve can have a variety of physical and mental health benefits, including improving mood, reducing stress, anxiety, and depression, improving cognitive functions and memory, lowering blood pressure and heart rate, boosting the immune system and fighting inflammation, promoting digestion and metabolism, and regulating the nervous system.

Vagus Nerve and Inflammatory Reaction

The vagus nerve and the inflammatory response are both critical components of your health and well-being. The inflammatory response is your body's natural and protective strategy for fighting diseases and injuries. It includes the activation and release of immune cells and chemicals, such as cytokines, which aid in the elimination of infections and foreign substances.

However, the inflammatory response can become exaggerated or persistent, resulting in tissue damage and illness. This can occur if your body is subjected to prolonged or recurrent stress, toxins, allergies, or infections. Examples of inflammatory disorders include rheumatoid arthritis, Crohn's disease, diabetes, and cancer. These illnesses can cause pain, swelling, redness, heat, and loss of function in the afflicted organs and tissues.

The vagus nerve can help control and balance the inflammatory response by transmitting and receiving information between your brain and immune system. This is known as the inflammatory reflex, and it works as follows: when your immune cells sense a threat, they transmit messages to your brain through the vagus nerve. Your brain then sends instructions to your immune cells via the vagus nerve, instructing them to limit the synthesis and release of cytokines and other inflammatory substances. This allows your body to regulate the inflammation and keep it from causing injury.

Stimulating the vagus nerve can boost the inflammatory response and improve your overall health and well-being. You can stimulate your vagus nerve naturally or with technology, depending on your requirements and preferences.

Stimulating the vagus nerve can provide a variety of advantages, including:
- Enhancing your mood while lowering stress, anxiety, and sadness. The vagus nerve connects your brain and intestines, releasing chemicals that influence your emotions. Stimulating the vagus nerve boosts levels of serotonin and dopamine, linked to pleasure and well-being[12].
- Increasing your cognitive abilities and memory. The vagus nerve also connects the brain to the ears, which are responsible for hearing and language. Stimulating the vagus nerve enhances auditory processing, linguistic capabilities, and learning abilities[3].
- Reducing your blood pressure and heart rate. The vagus nerve controls your cardiovascular system by providing messages to the heart and

blood vessels. Stimulating the vagus nerve activates the parasympathetic nervous system, which relaxes the body and lowers blood pressure and heart rate.

- Boosting your immune system and reducing inflammation. The vagus nerve controls your immune system and inflammation by providing signals to your spleen, lymph nodes, and bone marrow. Stimulating the vagus nerve increases immune cell synthesis and activity while decreasing cytokines and other inflammatory chemicals.

Chapter 2: The Vagus Nerve and Stress

How does stress influence the vagus nerve and vice versa?

Stress is a normal and inescapable aspect of life. It can be caused by a number of causes, including employment, relationships, health, and finances. Stress may have a beneficial and bad impact on both your health and psyche. It may help you deal with difficult situations, drive you to perform better, and improve your learning and memory. However, it may be harmful to your health and well-being, particularly if it is chronic or excessive. Stress may cause or aggravate a variety of medical and mental diseases, including heart disease, diabetes, depression, and anxiety.

Stress may influence your health in a variety of ways, including altering your vagus nerve. Depending on the scenario, the vagus nerve allows your body to flip between fight-or-flight and rest-and-digest mode. The fight-or-flight reaction gets your body ready for action by raising awareness, energy, and blood supply to the muscles. The rest-and-digest mode relaxes your body, lowering your heart rate, blood pressure, and stress levels.

Stress can impact the vagus nerve both directly and indirectly. Stress can directly stimulate or inhibit the vagus nerve, depending on its nature, severity, and length. Acute stress, for example, can activate the vagus nerve, resulting in a brief dip in blood pressure and heart rate that might cause dizziness or fainting. The vasovagal response is a defensive mechanism that keeps you from overexerting yourself. However, persistent stress might inhibit the vagus nerve's capacity to relax your body and mind. This can result in a condition of continual alertness, increasing your risk of cardiovascular and metabolic disorders.

Stress can indirectly impact the vagus nerve by causing changes in the amounts of hormones and neurotransmitters it interacts with. Stress, for example, can raise cortisol, adrenaline, and noradrenaline levels, all of which promote the fight-or-flight response. These hormones can disrupt the vagus nerve's function, making it difficult for your body to rest and recuperate. Stress can also reduce the levels of serotonin, dopamine, and GABA, neurotransmitters that govern mood, behavior, and cognition. These neurotransmitters can alter the function of the vagus nerve, allowing your body to cope better with stress and emotions.

The vagus nerve can influence stress in two ways: directly and indirectly. The vagus nerve directly reduces stress by activating the rest-and-digest mode, which decreases your heart rate, blood pressure, and stress levels. The vagus nerve can also alleviate stress by promoting the creation and release of substances like acetylcholine, norepinephrine, and cytokines, which combat inflammation and promote healing. These compounds can help your body cope with illnesses and injuries, both of which can be stressful. Indirectly, the vagus nerve can alleviate stress by altering mood and emotion. The vagus nerve can boost the amounts of neurotransmitters such as serotonin, dopamine, and GABA, which improve your pleasure and well-being. The vagus nerve can also affect your social and emotional abilities, such as empathy, compassion, and communication. These abilities can assist you in developing healthy relationships, which can protect you from stress.

As a result, the vagus nerve and stress interact in a bidirectional and complicated manner. Depending on the circumstances, they might have both good and negative effects on one another. By stimulating your vagus nerve, you can boost its function and get the advantages.

The vagus nerve and the hypothalamic-pituitary-adrenal (HPA) axis

The vagus nerve and the hypothalamic-pituitary-adrenal (HPA) axis are two critical systems that assist your body deal with stress and maintain equilibrium. They are physically and functionally linked, and they impact one another in a variety of ways. Here's a detailed explanation of the vagus nerve and the HPA axis, as well as their relationship to your health and well-being.

It starts in the brain stem and leaves the skull via the jugular foramen. It then passes through the neck, chest, and belly, releasing different branches along the route.

The HPA axis is a complex network of hormones and glands that regulates the stress response and circadian rhythm. It is made up of three primary parts: the hypothalamus, pituitary gland, and adrenal glands. The hypothalamus is a tiny region in the brain that controls numerous bodily activities, including temperature, hunger, and sleep. The pituitary gland is a pea-sized gland at the base of the brain that generates and secretes hormones that influence growth, metabolism, reproduction, and stress. The adrenal glands are two triangular-shaped glands located on top of the kidneys. They generate and emit chemicals that influence the fight-or-flight response, including cortisol, adrenaline, and noradrenaline.

When your body detects a stressful condition, such as a danger, a challenge, or a change, the HPA axis is triggered. It initiates a chain of actions that prime your body for action or adaptability. The hypothalamus secretes corticotropin-releasing hormone (CRH), which causes the pituitary gland to secrete adrenocorticotropic hormone (ACTH). ACTH goes through the circulation to the adrenal glands, which respond by generating and releasing cortisol, the primary stress hormone. Cortisol has a variety of impacts on the body, including boosting blood sugar, blood pressure, and heart rate, inhibiting the immune system and inflammation, and improving memory and alertness. Cortisol also works as a negative feedback mechanism, limiting the production of CRH and ACTH while returning the HPA axis to its normal condition.

The vagus nerve can influence the HPA axis and the stress response by transmitting and receiving messages between the brain and the body. The vagus nerve can either stimulate or suppress the HPA axis, depending on the kind, severity, and duration of the stressor. For example, modest or acute stress can stimulate the vagus nerve, enhancing the HPA axis and cortisol response and assisting the body in dealing with the stressor. However, severe or persistent stress can suppress the vagus nerve, impairing the HPA axis and cortisol response and causing the body to suffer as a result of the stressor. The vagus nerve can also have an indirect effect on the HPA axis by affecting hormone and neurotransmitter levels. The vagus nerve, for example, can boost levels of serotonin, dopamine, and GABA, all of which are neurotransmitters that affect mood, behavior, and cognition. These neurotransmitters can regulate the HPA axis and cortisol response, lowering stress, anxiety, and depression.

The vagus nerve and the cortisol response and The vagus nerve and the immune system

The vagus nerve and the cortisol response are two mechanisms that assist the body in dealing with stress. The cortisol response is a chemical reaction that primes your body for action and adaptability. It is primarily regulated by the hypothalamic-pituitary-adrenal (HPA) axis, which is made up of three glands: the hypothalamus, pituitary, and adrenal glands.

When confronted with a stressful event, such as a danger, challenge, or change, your body stimulates both the vagus nerve and the cortisol response. The vagus nerve prompts your heart, lungs, and digestive system to slow down or speed up, depending on your demands. It also prompts your brain to release hormones that alleviate pain and anxiety. The cortisol response causes a rise in cortisol, adrenaline, and noradrenaline levels, all of which raise blood sugar, blood pressure, and heart rate. They also lower your immune system and inflammation while improving your memory and attentiveness.

The vagus nerve and the cortisol response work together to help you cope with stress, but they may also have severe consequences if they are hyperactive or inactive. Excessive vagus nerve activity can result in low blood pressure, fainting, and organ damage. Too much cortisol response can lead to excessive blood pressure, diabetes, obesity, and depression. Inadequate vagus nerve activation can result in chronic inflammation, autoimmune illnesses, and mental issues. Inadequate cortisol response might result in weariness, weakness, or low blood sugar.

The vagus nerve and the immune system are also two systems that assist your body in fighting infections and injuries. The vagus nerve is a component of the inflammatory reflex, which controls the immune system and inflammation. The immune system is a network of cells and chemicals that defends the body against diseases and other substances. Inflammation is the activation and release of immune cells and chemicals, such as cytokines, to assist eradicate infections and foreign substances.

When your immune system recognizes a threat, such as bacteria, a virus, or a wound, it initiates inflammation to combat it. However, severe or persistent inflammation can lead to tissue damage and illness. This can occur if your body is subjected to prolonged or recurrent stress, toxins, allergies, or infections. Examples of inflammatory disorders include rheumatoid arthritis, Crohn's disease, diabetes, and cancer. These illnesses can cause pain, swelling, redness, heat, and loss of function in the afflicted organs and tissues.

The vagus nerve, which sends and receives messages between the brain and the body, can help control and balance the immune system and reduce inflammation. The vagus nerve may either stimulate or suppress the immune system and inflammation, depending on the kind, severity, and duration of the danger. For example, moderate or acute inflammation can stimulate the vagus nerve, boosting the immune system and inflammation and assisting the body in fighting the threat. Severe or chronic inflammation, on the other hand, can suppress the vagus nerve, impairing the immune system and inflammation and making the body vulnerable to the threat. The vagus nerve can also have an indirect effect on the immune system and inflammation by affecting hormone and neurotransmitter levels that interact with them. For example, the vagus nerve can boost levels of acetylcholine, norepinephrine, and cytokines, which are substances that combat inflammation and promote healing.

Chapter 3: The Vagus Nerve and Mental Health

Vagus Nerve and Mental Problems

The vagus nerve and mood disorders are two issues that concern your mental health and well-being. Mood disorders are a class of mental diseases that influence your mood, feelings, and behavior. Mood disorders include depression, bipolar disorder, and anxiety disorder.

The vagus nerve influences your mood and emotions by transmitting and receiving messages between your brain and your body. The vagus nerve can influence the synthesis and function of neurotransmitters including serotonin, dopamine, and GABA, which govern mood, behavior, and cognition. The vagus nerve can also influence the action of the hypothalamic-pituitary-adrenal (HPA) axis, a network of hormones and glands that regulates stress and cortisol levels. The vagus nerve can also alter immune system function and inflammation, both of which can influence your mood and emotions.

The vagus nerve can help prevent or cure mood problems by activating or toning the parasympathetic nervous system, bringing your body and mind back into balance and calm. Stimulating the vagus nerve can boost serotonin, dopamine, and GABA levels, improving your mood and well-being. Stimulating the vagus nerve can also lower cortisol, adrenaline, and noradrenaline levels, so reducing stress, anxiety, and depression. Stimulating the vagus nerve can also boost the synthesis and activity of immune cells and chemicals including acetylcholine, norepinephrine, and cytokines, which can combat inflammation and improve healing.

Vagus Nerve and Anxiety Disorders

The vagus nerve and anxiety disorders are two issues that concern your mental health and well-being. Anxiety disorders are a type of mental disease characterized by excessive dread, uneasiness, or concern in a variety of settings. Anxiety disorders include generalised anxiety disorder, panic disorder, social anxiety disorder, and phobias.

The vagus nerve influences your anxiety levels by controlling your stress response and inflammation. The stress response is a physiological process that prepares your body to take action or adapt in the face of a threat or challenge. Inflammation is the process by which immune cells and molecules are activated and released to assist eradicate infections and foreign substances.

Anxiety causes your stress response and inflammation to become hyperactive or persistent, resulting in physical and emotional difficulties. Your heart rate, blood pressure, and respiration might all increase, while your immune system and digestion can suffer, as well as your mood and cognition. This can increase your anxiety, fear, or worry, creating a vicious cycle.

The vagus nerve can assist stop this cycle by activating or tuning the parasympathetic nervous system, bringing your body and mind back into balance and calmness. Stimulating the vagus nerve can reduce your heart rate, blood pressure, and respiration, boost your immune system and digestion, and improve your mood and cognitive abilities. This can help you feel more calm, confident, and cheerful, resulting in a positive cycle.

The Vagus Nerve and PTSD

The vagus nerve and post-traumatic stress disorder (PTSD) are two issues that concern your mental health and well-being. PTSD is a mental condition that develops following a stressful incident, such as a war, natural catastrophe, attack, or accident. When people with PTSD are reminded of the event, they frequently have nightmares, flashbacks, intrusive thoughts, and feelings of discomfort. They may also avoid events, locations, or people that bring up memories. They may experience numbness, detachment, anger, or guilt. They may have difficulty sleeping, focusing, or interacting with others.

When you experience a traumatic incident, your stress response and inflammation might become hyperactive or chronic, resulting in physical and mental health issues. Your heart rate, blood pressure, and respiration might all increase, while your immune system and digestion can suffer, as well as your mood and cognition. This can lead to increased anxiety, fear, and depression, creating a vicious cycle.

The vagus nerve can assist stop this cycle by activating or tuning the parasympathetic nervous system, bringing your body and mind back into balance and calmness.

Vagus Nerve and Cognitive Functioning

Memory, learning, attention, and language are among the cognitive activities that the vagus nerve regulates.

The vagus nerve can influence cognitive functions via regulating the activity of brain areas and chemicals involved in cognition. For example, the vagus nerve can trigger the production of acetylcholine, a neurotransmitter that improves memory and learning. The vagus nerve can also stimulate the hippocampus, a brain area involved for memory creation and consolidation. The vagus nerve can also affect the prefrontal cortex, a brain area involved in attention, decision-making, and executive processes. The vagus nerve can also impact the auditory cortex, a brain area responsible for hearing and language processing.

Chapter 4: "The Vagus Nerve and Physical Health"

Vagus nerve and cardiovascular health.

The vagus nerve, a key component of the parasympathetic nervous system, has a considerable impact on the heart and cardiovascular system. It works with the sympathetic nervous system to control heart rate and is critical in maintaining physiological homeostasis. The complicated interplay between the vagus nerve and the cardiovascular system emphasizes the close relationship between our mental and physical well-being.

Vagus nerve stimulation (VNS) has been shown in studies to be effective in treating a variety of cardiovascular disorders, including heart failure, cardiac arrest, acute myocardial infarction, and stroke. The vagus nerve's innervation of the heart has established VNS as a possible treatment option for cardiovascular problems. Studies have shown a relationship between vagus nerve activity and the high-frequency component of heart rate variability, which corresponds with vagal tone, highlighting the nerve's role in cardiovascular function.

VNS has been studied for its ability to reduce intrinsic cardiac neurons and unfavorable myocyte remodeling, providing insight into its protective role against myocardial ischemia/reperfusion damage. These findings highlight the far-reaching consequences of VNS in maintaining cardiovascular health.

Furthermore, the vagus nerve's role in physiological homeostasis, which includes reflex circuits that control heart function, emphasizes its importance in sustaining cardiovascular health. The potential use of VNS in the context of the cardiovascular system is now being investigated in preclinical and clinical settings, highlighting the growing interest in harnessing the vagus nerve's therapeutic potential for cardiovascular health.

Damage to the vagus nerve can cause a variety of symptoms, including heart rate abnormalities, highlighting the nerve's critical role in cardiovascular function. This demonstrates the vagus nerve's enormous influence on our physical well-being, as well as the complicated relationship between our emotions and body functions.

In essence, the vagus nerve's extensive impact on the heart and circulatory system emphasizes its critical role in maintaining physiological balance and cardiovascular health. The current investigation into the possible uses of VNS for cardiovascular problems reflects the rising acknowledgment of the vagus nerve as an important factor in maintaining our cardiovascular health. This complicated interplay between the vagus nerve and the circulatory system not only illuminates the physiological mechanisms at work, but it also emphasizes the intimate connection between our emotional and physical experiences.

Vagus nerve and intestinal health.

The vagus nerve is your gut's best friend.
Consider your stomach to be a lively bazaar, full with activity. A complex network of nerves,

muscles, and organs transports food, breaks it down, absorbs nutrients, and eliminates waste. But have you heard about the hidden VIP in this operation? Enter the vagus nerve, your body's personal "gut guru."

Think of the vagus nerve as a superhighway that connects your brain and intestines. It's like a two-way street, with messages continually flowing back and forth, impacting everything from digestion to mood. But what makes it so beneficial to your gut health?

The Calming Conductor:
Have you ever felt butterflies in your stomach during a presentation? Your nervous system is sending stress signals down the line. The vagus nerve can operate as a conductor, relaxing these impulses and enabling more efficient digestion transit. When triggered, it can do:

Slow your pulse rate: Imagine a softer heartbeat, similar to peaceful music, rather than a drum solo, allowing your gut to focus on its work.

Relax your muscles: Tense muscles can impede digestion, but the vagus nerve can ease them up for more effective processing.

Increase blood flow: Similar to sending more workers to the market, higher blood flow allows your intestines to absorb nutrients more effectively.

The Gut Feeling Guru:

However, the vagus nerve does more than merely slow things down. It's also a two-way street, transporting information from your gut to your brain. This gut-brain link is essential for recognizing your body's demands and fostering general health.

Hunger pangs: Do you feel a growl in your stomach? The vagus nerve may be delivering a message to your brain, suggesting, "Hey, time to refuel!"

Food satisfaction: Do you feel full and pleased after a meal? The vagus nerve might be assisting your brain in recognizing that you've had enough.

Mood and emotions: Did you know that your stomach may affect your mood? The vagus nerve plays a part in this relationship, allowing you to feel calm and balanced.

Activate Your Inner Guru:
So, how can you harness the power of the vagus nerve to improve your gut health? Here are some entertaining and engaging approaches:

Deep breathing: Take slow, deliberate breaths. Imagine each breath as a soft wave that massages your belly.

Mindfulness and meditation: Relax your thoughts and reconnect with your body. Imagine your belly is quiet and content.

Singing and humming cause vibrations that activate the vagus nerve, encouraging relaxation and digestion.

Yoga and mild movement: Stretching and movement can help stimulate the vagus nerve and increase gastrointestinal motility.

Spending time outdoors can help decrease stress and improve intestinal health.

Remember that everyone's body is unique, so what works for one person may not work for another. It is usually advisable to contact a healthcare practitioner before beginning any new practices, especially if you have any underlying health issues.

Understanding and activating your vagus nerve allows your stomach to operate efficiently, resulting in a happier and healthier you! So, trust your instincts, engage your inner guru, and begin on a path of wellness!

Vagus Nerve and Respiratory Health

The vagus nerve and respiratory health are two areas that are intimately linked to your well-being.

The vagus nerve can impact your respiratory health by regulating or affecting respiration and airway tightness. The vagus nerve provides messages to your lungs and bronchi to change your breathing rate and depth based on your oxygen and carbon dioxide levels. It also regulates the muscles in your airways, allowing them to contract or relax. A healthy vagus nerve can help prevent or cure respiratory illnesses including asthma, COPD, and sleep apnea[12].

The vagus nerve can also assist prevent or treat respiratory infections and inflammation by controlling the immune system and the inflammatory response. The immune system is a network of cells and chemicals that defends the body against diseases and other substances. The inflammatory reflex is a mechanism that controls the immune system and inflammation by transmitting and receiving signals between the brain and the body. The vagus nerve detects and responds to infections and lesions in the lungs by delivering signals to produce chemicals that combat inflammation and promote healing. It also affects the functioning of immunological cells like macrophages and lymphocytes, which aid in the elimination of infections and foreign substances. A healthy vagus nerve can help you avoid chronic inflammatory disorders including pneumonia, bronchitis, and TB.

Vagus nerve and metabolic health

Metabolic health refers to the state of having a healthy metabolism, which is the process by which food is converted into energy and used for various biological tasks. Metabolic health is critical for keeping a healthy weight, blood sugar, blood pressure, and cholesterol. Many variables influence metabolic health, including nutrition, exercise, genetics, and hormones.

The vagus nerve is important for metabolic health because it connects the brain to several metabolism-related organs and systems, including the stomach, intestines, pancreas, liver, and kidneys. The vagus nerve can affect metabolic health in the following ways:

- Increasing the synthesis and release of digestive juices and hormones, which aid in the breakdown and absorption of food, as well as the regulation of hunger and blood sugar levels.
- Controlling the flow of food through the digestive system and the elimination of waste items from the body.
- Controlling the action of the hypothalamic-pituitary-adrenal (HPA) axis, a

network of hormones and glands that regulates stress and cortisol levels. Cortisol is a hormone that regulates blood sugar, blood pressure, and inflammation.

- Changing the immune system and inflammation, which can impact blood sugar, blood pressure, and cholesterol levels.

Chapter 5: How to Naturally Stimulate the Vagus Nerve

Breathing exercises and strategies.

Breathing exercises and methods are one of the most simple and efficient ways to activate your vagus nerve organically. Breathing is an instinctive function regulated by the vagus nerve, but you may deliberately alter your breathing pattern to impact vagus nerve activity. Deep, calm, and rhythmic breathing helps improve heart rate variability and vagus nerve function.

To naturally activate your vagus nerve, try the following breathing exercises and techniques:
- Diaphragmatic breathing. This is a style of breathing that uses your diaphragm, a big muscle located at the base of your lungs. To practice diaphragmatic breathing, lie on your

back or sit comfortably. Place one hand on your chest, the other on your abdomen. Inhale via your nose, filling your belly with air. You should feel your abdomen rise while your chest stays stationary. Exhale via your lips, emptying your abdomen of air. You should feel your abdomen descend while your chest stays stationary. Repeat for a few minutes, focusing on your breathing. Diaphragmatic breathing can help you relax, relieve tension, and lower blood pressure.

- Resonant breathing. This is a style of breathing in which you breathe at a pace of roughly six breaths per minute, which is the best frequency for activating the vagus nerve. To practice resonant breathing, sit comfortably and inhale through your nose for around five seconds. Exhale through your lips for roughly five seconds. Try to keep your inhalations and exhalations smooth and even. Repeat for a few minutes, focusing on your breathing. Resonant breathing can help you relax, elevate your mood, and increase your cognitive abilities.

- Breathe through each nostril alternately. This is a sort of breathing in which you alternate between your nostrils, which can help to balance the activity of your left and right brain and neurological system. To practice alternating nostril breathing, sit comfortably and seal your right nostril with your thumb. Inhale via your left nostril for approximately four seconds. Hold your breath for around four seconds. Close your left nostril with your right ring finger, then release your right thumb. Exhale via your right nostril for roughly four seconds. Inhale via your right nostril for approximately four seconds. Hold your breath for around four seconds. Close your right nose with your thumb and then release your right ring finger. Exhale via your left nostril for roughly four seconds. This completes a single cycle. Repeat this numerous times, focusing on your breath. Alternate nostril breathing can help you relax, reduce anxiety, and improve concentration and awareness.

These are some breathing exercises and strategies that can help activate your vagus nerve organically. You can practice them wherever and anywhere you choose, as long as you're comfortable and secure. You may also combine them with other natural ways to stimulate your vagus nerve, such as meditation, yoga, singing, or humming. These techniques can help you relax, unwind, and improve your health and well-being.

Meditation and mindfulness methods

Meditation and mindfulness activities are among the most effective methods to naturally activate the vagus nerve. Meditation is the technique of focusing your attention on a single object, such as your breath, a mantra, or a sound. Mindfulness is a discipline that requires focusing on the present moment without judgment or distraction. Meditation and mindfulness are also effective methods for relaxing, calming, and reducing stress and inflammation.

- Breathing awareness meditation. This is a sort of meditation in which you observe your normal breathing rhythm without attempting to modify or control it. To practice breath awareness meditation, sit comfortably and close your eyes. Pay attention to how your breath moves in and out of your nostrils. Feel the feelings of breathing in your nose, chest, and abdomen. If your thoughts wander, gently bring them back to your breath. Do this for 10 to 20 minutes, or until you feel comfortable. Breath awareness meditation can help you relax, reduce your heart rate and blood pressure, and improve your vagal tone.

- Practice loving-kindness meditation. This is a sort of meditation in which you cultivate positive sentiments of love, compassion, and goodwill for yourself and others. To practice loving-kindness meditation, sit comfortably and close your eyes. Begin by focusing your attention on your heart, and experience a warm and calm sensation there. Then, repeat the following sentences quietly or loudly, directing them to yourself: "May I be happy. May I be healthy. May I be safe. May I be at peace.\" Feel the significance of these words in your heart and wish yourself well. Next, address the same sentences to someone you care about, such as a family member, a friend, or a pet. Feel the connection and affection you share with this person, and wish them well. Then, say the same lines to someone you feel indifferent towards, such as a neighbor, coworker, or stranger. Feel your regard and care for this individual, and wish them the best. Finally, repeat the same sentences while directing them at someone you disagree with, such as an opponent, a rival, or a critic. Feel your forgiveness and compassion for this individual, and wish them the best. Extend your loving-kindness to all creatures by repeating the phrases: \"May all beings be happy. May all beings be healthy. May all beings be safe. May all beings be at peace.\" Repeat for 10 to 20 minutes, or as long as you feel comfortable. Loving-kindness meditation can boost your mood, reduce anxiety and sadness, and improve your social and emotional abilities.

- **Practice body scan awareness**. This is a sort of mindfulness practice in which you focus on your body's sensations without judgment or reaction. To practice body scan awareness, lie on your back or in a comfortable seat. Close your eyes and take several deep breaths. Then, focus your attention on your feet and take note of any feelings you feel, such as warmth, cold, tingling, or pressure. Observe these sensations with curiosity and acceptance, without attempting to modify or avoid them. Then, focus your attention on your lower legs and repeat the process. Continue scanning your body, including your knees, thighs, hips, lower and upper backs, chest, belly, shoulders, arms, hands, neck, face, and head. Pay attention to each portion of your body and note any sensations you feel, such as pain, stress, relaxation, or pleasure. Observe these sensations with curiosity and acceptance, without attempting to modify or avoid them. Do this for 10 to 20 minutes, or until you feel comfortable. Body scan mindfulness can help you relax, reduce pain and inflammation, and increase body awareness and self-regulation.

Yoga and other physical exercises.

Imagine your body as a buzzing orchestra, with each organ contributing to the melody of life. However, the conductor's tension might cause the music to become disorganized. Enter the vagus nerve, your body's "chill conductor," which calms things down and restores harmony to the scene.

So, how can you lead your own internal orchestra and harness the power of the vagus nerve? Prepare to release your inner chill with these fun and natural activities:

Yoga: Visualize yourself flowing through positions like a graceful dancer, breathing in time with the action. Yoga positions such as child's pose, forward folds, and mild twists can help stimulate the vagus nerve by squeezing your belly and activating certain neural pathways. Consider each exhalation a sigh of relief, releasing tension and welcoming peace.

Deep breathing: Inhale deeply through your nose, feeling your stomach expand like a balloon. Hold for a few seconds before gently exhaling, visualizing stress melting away with each breath. This simple yet effective approach provides soothing impulses to the vagus nerve, which promotes relaxation and lowers your heart rate. Consider it a mental and physical "pause" button.

Humming and Chanting: Visualize the calm vibrations of your hum echoing throughout your body like a comforting lullaby. Humming and chanting stimulate the vagus nerve via vocal cord vibrations, increasing relaxation and lowering tension. Consider it a mini-internal massage that soothes your nervous system and promotes relaxation.

Progressive Muscle Relaxation: Tense and release different muscle groups, beginning with your toes and progressing up. Pay attention to how tension leaves your body as you relax each muscle group. This approach reduces total body tension, stimulating the vagus nerve and promoting feelings of relaxation. Consider each release as a wave that washes away stress, leaving you feeling lighter and more relaxed.

Mindfulness & Meditation: Locate a peaceful area, close your eyes, and concentrate on the present moment. Without passing judgment, pay attention to your breathing, physical sensations, and thoughts. Mindfulness and meditation assist to calm the mind and stimulate the parasympathetic nervous system, which includes the vagus nerve. Imagine your thoughts becoming as peaceful as a serene lake, reflecting the beauty of the present moment.

Spending Time in Nature: Take a stroll around the park, feel the sun on your skin, and listen to the sounds of nature. Immersion in nature has been found to alleviate stress and stimulate the vagus nerve. Imagine fresh air entering your lungs, the sun warming your body, and the sounds of nature soothing your mind. It functions as a natural reset button for your neurological system.

Singing, Humming, and Chanting

- **Singing.** Singing is an excellent method to express oneself and appreciate music. Singing stimulates your vagus nerve by engaging your voice cords and diaphragm, lowering your heart rate and blood pressure while improving breathing and oxygen supply. Singing can also activate your vagus nerve, producing neurotransmitters like serotonin, dopamine, and oxytocin, which can boost your mood and social skills. Singing can also activate your vagus nerve by syncing your brain waves and heart rate with others around you, which can improve empathy and connection. You can sing solo or with others, in the shower or in a chorus, with or without music, as long as you enjoy it and feel wonderful.

- **Humming.** Humming is a simple approach to activate the vagus nerve. Humming stimulates your vagus nerve by causing sound vibrations to engage your voice cords and throat muscles, lowering your heart rate and blood pressure while improving your breathing and oxygen supply. Humming can also activate your vagus nerve, producing neurotransmitters like serotonin, dopamine, and oxytocin, which can boost your mood and well-being. Humming can also activate the vagus nerve by matching your brain waves and pulse rate with others, improving communication and connection. You may hum whenever and wherever you choose, with or without music, as long as you're comfortable and tranquil.

- **Chanting.** Chanting is an effective and traditional approach to activate the vagus nerve. Chanting can stimulate the vagus nerve by causing sound vibrations to engage your voice cords and throat muscles, lowering your heart rate and blood pressure while improving your breathing and oxygen supply. Chanting can also activate your vagus nerve, producing neurotransmitters like serotonin, dopamine, and oxytocin, which can boost your mood and spirituality. Chanting can also activate your vagus nerve by syncing your brain waves and heart rate with those of others, which can help you meditate and transcend. You can chant alone or with others, with or without music, using words or sounds like mantras, prayers, or om, as long as you are focused and connected.

Chapter 6: How to Stimulate the Vagus Nerve with Technology

Transcutaneous vagus nerve stimulation (tVNS)

tVNS is a non-invasive and safe technique that can stimulate the vagus nerve, which is a key component of your nervous system that affects your physical and mental health. By stimulating the vagus nerve, tVNS can modulate a variety of physiological processes, such as inflammation, pain, heart rate, blood pressure, digestion, and more. In this explanation, I will tell you more about what tVNS is, how it works, and what its potential benefits and applications are.

What is tVNS?
tVNS is a form of nerve stimulation that involves applying electrical pulses to the skin overlying the vagus nerve, which runs from the brainstem down through the neck and into the chest and abdomen. Unlike invasive forms of

vagus nerve stimulation, such as surgically implanted devices, tVNS uses electrodes placed on the skin to deliver low-level electrical currents to the nerve. One of the main benefits of tVNS is its non-invasive nature, which allows for repeated use over time without the need for surgery. Additionally, tVNS is generally considered to be safe and well-tolerated, with few significant side effects reported in the literature[12].

How does tVNS work?

tVNS works by stimulating the vagus nerve.

By stimulating the vagus nerve, tVNS can activate the parasympathetic nervous system, which can restore your body and mind to a state of balance and calm. Stimulating the vagus nerve can lower your heart rate, blood pressure, and breathing, improve your immune system and digestion, and enhance your mood and cognition. This can make you feel more relaxed, confident, and happy, creating a positive cycle.

What are the potential benefits and applications of tVNS?

tVNS has been shown to have a range of potential therapeutic applications, for various conditions that involve the vagus nerve, the parasympathetic nervous system, or the inflammatory reflex. Some of these conditions include:

- Chronic pain. Chronic pain is a condition where pain persists for more than three months, and is often associated with inflammation, stress, and depression. tVNS can help reduce chronic pain, by modulating the pain signals in the brain and spinal cord, and by reducing inflammation and stress[34].
- Depression. Depression is a mood disorder that causes persistent feelings of sadness, hopelessness, and loss of interest. tVNS can help treat depression, by stimulating the release of neurotransmitters, such as serotonin, dopamine, and noradrenaline, which can improve mood and motivation. tVNS can also stimulate the activity of brain regions, such as the prefrontal cortex and the hippocampus, which are involved in emotion regulation and memory formation .
- Epilepsy. Epilepsy is a neurological disorder that causes recurrent seizures, which are sudden and abnormal bursts of electrical activity in the brain. tVNS can help prevent or reduce

seizures, by stabilizing the brain activity and inhibiting the seizure onset and propagation .

- Migraine. Migraine is a type of headache that causes severe and throbbing pain, often accompanied by nausea, vomiting, and sensitivity to light and sound. tVNS can help relieve migraine, by blocking the activation of the trigeminal nerve, which is a major source of pain and inflammation in migraine. tVNS can also reduce the frequency and intensity of migraine attacks, by modulating the brainstem and the hypothalamus, which are involved in migraine generation and regulation .

Auricular vagus nerve stimulation (aVNS)

Auricular Vagus Nerve Stimulation (aVNS) is an innovative approach that involves the non-invasive electrical stimulation of the auricular branch of the vagus nerve, which is located in the ear. This emerging technology has garnered significant attention due to its potential therapeutic applications in various physiological processes and medical conditions. By targeting the vagus nerve, aVNS modulates afferent vagus nerve activity, influencing a wide array of bodily functions and offering promising prospects for the treatment of inflammatory, cardiovascular, and neurodegenerative disease.

The procedure for aVNS typically involves the placement of electrodes or miniature needles in the concha and/or the inferior part of the ear. These electrodes are connected to a stimulation device, and the stimulation is often performed at the tragus or concha. The aVNS approach is non-invasive, with few side effects and contraindications, making it a well-tolerated and safe intervention for patients. The stimulation is usually administered daily, with intervals of at least 3 hours between sessions, and it has been suggested as a potential co-adjuvant treatment for inflammatory manifestations, although further clinical studies are needed to establish its efficacy conclusively.

The physiological perspective of aVNS underscores its potential to influence disease processes and therapeutic outcomes. Studies have demonstrated its effects on a wide range of conditions, including peripheral arterial occlusive disease, cardiovascular diseases, and inflammatory ailments. The modulatory effects of aVNS on the vagus nerve activity have shown promise in improving symptoms and mitigating disease processes, highlighting its potential as a sustainable therapeutic approach.

The link between aVNS and inflammation in cardiovascular diseases has been a subject of particular interest. Research has indicated that vagus nerve stimulation, including aVNS, may have a role in modulating inflammation in the context of cardiovascular conditions. The parasympathetic nervous system, through the vagus nerve, exerts a profound influence over the heart, and the potential of aVNS to impact inflammatory processes in cardiovascular diseases has been a focus of ongoing investigation.

While the potential of aVNS in various medical conditions is promising, further studies are needed to elucidate the underlying mechanisms and establish its clinical significance conclusively. The emerging evidence from case series and clinical trials provides valuable insights into the potential of aVNS as a multimodal therapeutic concept, contributing to a better understanding of its therapeutic applications and the need for further research to validate its efficacy

Invasive vagus nerve stimulation (iVNS)

Invasive Vagus Nerve Stimulation (iVNS) is a medical procedure that involves the surgical implantation of a device that delivers electrical stimulation to the vagus nerve. The procedure is typically reserved for patients with severe and treatment-resistant conditions, such as epilepsy, depression, and chronic pain. The device is implanted in the chest, and the electrical stimulation is delivered through wires that are connected to the vagus nerve. The stimulation is typically administered at regular intervals, and the device can be programmed to deliver different levels of stimulation based on the patient's needs.

The physiological perspective of iVNS underscores its potential to influence disease processes and therapeutic outcomes. Studies have demonstrated its effects on a wide range of conditions, including epilepsy, depression, and chronic pain. The modulatory effects of iVNS on the vagus nerve activity have shown promise in improving symptoms and mitigating disease processes, highlighting its potential as a sustainable therapeutic approach.

The link between iVNS and inflammation in cardiovascular diseases has been a subject of particular interest. Research has indicated that vagus nerve stimulation, including iVNS, may have a role in modulating inflammation in the context of cardiovascular conditions. The parasympathetic nervous system, through the vagus nerve, exerts a profound influence over the heart, and the potential of iVNS to impact inflammatory processes in cardiovascular diseases has been a focus of ongoing investigation.

While the potential of iVNS in various medical conditions is promising, the procedure is invasive and carries risks associated with surgery. The device can malfunction, and the wires can become dislodged, leading to complications. Furthermore, the procedure is costly and may not be covered by insurance, making it inaccessible to many patients.

Biofeedback and neurofeedback devices

Biofeedback is a general term that refers to any technique that provides you with feedback on your biological functions, such as your blood pressure, skin temperature, or breathing rate. Biofeedback devices can measure these functions using sensors attached to your body, and display them on a screen or through sounds. By observing these signals, you can learn to recognize and change your body's responses to stress, pain, or emotions. For example, you can use biofeedback to lower your heart rate and blood pressure, relax your muscles, or reduce your headaches.

Neurofeedback is a specific type of biofeedback that provides feedback directly on brain activity. Neurofeedback devices can measure your brain waves using electrodes attached to your scalp, and display them on a screen or through sounds. By observing these signals, you can learn to modify your brain activity and enhance your cognitive functions, such as your attention, memory, or mood. For example, you can use neurofeedback to increase your alpha waves and decrease your beta waves, which can improve your relaxation and creativity.

There are many types of biofeedback and neurofeedback devices available on the market, ranging from basic to advanced, and from cheap to expensive. Some of the most popular and effective devices are:

- **Sens.ai:** This is a neuroadaptive system that combines heart rate variability training, neurofeedback, and photobiomodulation into a wearable device. It uses gel-free technology to measure your brain waves, and provides personalized programs to optimize your cognitive performance and well-being[5].
- **Muse S:** This is an EEG device that caters to meditation, mindfulness, and sleep optimization. It uses advanced signal processing to interpret your mental activity, and provides auditory feedback to guide you. It also

introduces specific programs for enhancing sleep quality.

- **Narbis:** This is a smart glasses device that leverages neurofeedback and NASA algorithms for real-time attention, relaxation, and distraction tracking. It monitors your brain waves and adjusts the tint of the glasses according to your focus level. It helps you improve your mental performance by training your brain to stay in the zone.

- **Braintap:** This is a headset device that combines light and sound therapy, guided meditation, and neurofeedback to create a holistic brain wellness experience. It synchronizes your brain waves and balances your brain hemispheres, while delivering positive affirmations and relaxing music.

- **Muse:** This is an EEG device that focuses on meditation and mindfulness. It measures your brain waves and provides real-time feedback through weather sounds. It helps you calm your mind and reduce stress and anxiety.

Chapter 7: How to Incorporate Vagus Nerve Stimulation into Your Daily Life

In this chapter, you will learn how to apply the principles and practices of vagus nerve stimulation to your daily life, in order to enhance your health and well-being. You will discover tips and strategies for optimal vagus nerve health, common pitfalls and challenges to avoid, how to measure and monitor your vagus nerve activity, and how to create a personalized vagus nerve stimulation plan.

Tips and Strategies for Optimal Vagus Nerve Health

The vagus nerve is a major nerve that connects the brain to various organs and influences our psychological and physical well-being. According to the polyvagal theory, proposed by Stephen Porges, the vagus nerve has three branches that correspond to three evolutionary stages and three behavioral strategies: the dorsal vagal complex, the ventral vagal complex, and the smart vagus. Each branch is associated with different physiological and emotional responses to the environment and social interactions.

The goal of vagus nerve stimulation is to regulate the nervous system and activate the ventral vagal complex and the social engagement system, which are responsible for emotional regulation, communication, and connection with others. By stimulating the vagus nerve, we can enhance our sense of safety, well-being, and trust, as well as improve our digestion, immunity, and healing.
There are many ways to stimulate the vagus nerve, both internally and externally.

Some of the tips and strategies for optimal vagus nerve health are:
- Breathing exercises, which can calm the sympathetic branch and activate the ventral vagal complex, by modulating the heart rate and breathing. Some examples of breathing exercises are deep breathing, diaphragmatic breathing, alternate nostril breathing, and box breathing.
- Yoga, meditation, or mindfulness, which can enhance the awareness and control of the body

and mind, by focusing on the present moment and sensations. Some examples of yoga, meditation, or mindfulness practices are hatha yoga, vinyasa yoga, transcendental meditation, mindfulness-based stress reduction, and body scan.

- Music, art, or other creative activities, which can stimulate the ventral vagal complex and the social engagement system, by expressing and sharing emotions and experiences. Some examples of music, art, or other creative activities are singing, playing an instrument, listening to music, painting, drawing, writing, or dancing.

- Physical activity, which can release the tension and energy accumulated by the sympathetic branch, by moving the body and muscles. Some examples of physical activity are walking, jogging, cycling, swimming, or lifting weights.

- Social support, which can activate the ventral vagal complex and the social engagement system, by co-regulating with others who are calm, supportive, and trustworthy. Some examples of social support are talking to a friend, family member, or therapist, joining a support group, volunteering, or participating in a community event.

- Therapy, which can help identify and process the sources of stress and trauma, by providing a safe and empathic space to explore and heal. Some examples of therapy are cognitive-behavioral therapy, eye movement desensitization and reprocessing, somatic experiencing, or polyvagal-informed therapy.

Common Pitfalls and Challenges to Avoid

While vagus nerve stimulation can have many benefits for our health and well-being, it is not a magic bullet or a quick fix. It requires consistent practice, patience, and perseverance, as well as awareness of the potential pitfalls and challenges that may arise along the way.

Let look at some common pitfall to a avoid:

- Overstimulation or understimulation, which can occur when we stimulate the vagus nerve too much or too little, resulting in adverse effects on our nervous system. Overstimulation can cause symptoms such as anxiety, agitation, nausea, or dizziness, while under stimulation can cause symptoms such as depression, fatigue, numbness, or detachment. To avoid overstimulation or understimulation, we need to find the right balance and intensity of vagus nerve stimulation that suits our individual needs and preferences, and adjust it accordingly as we progress.

- Resistance or avoidance, which can occur when we encounter difficulties or discomforts in stimulating the vagus nerve, such as fear, pain, shame, or guilt. Resistance or avoidance can prevent us from accessing the benefits of vagus nerve stimulation, as well as reinforce the negative patterns and beliefs that keep us stuck in a dysregulated state. To overcome resistance or avoidance, we need to acknowledge and accept our feelings and sensations, without judging or suppressing them, and gently guide ourselves to a more regulated and safe state.

- Expectations or comparisons, which can occur when we have unrealistic or rigid expectations of ourselves or others, or when we compare ourselves to others or to an ideal standard. Expectations or comparisons can create pressure, frustration, or disappointment, as well as undermine our confidence and motivation. To let go of expectations or comparisons, we need to appreciate and celebrate our own progress and achievements, no matter how small or slow, and recognize that everyone has their own pace and path of vagus nerve stimulation.

How to Measure and Monitor Your Vagus Nerve Activity

One of the ways to measure and monitor your vagus nerve activity is to use a device called a heart rate variability (HRV) monitor. HRV is a measure of the variation in the time intervals between consecutive heartbeats, which reflects the balance between the sympathetic and parasympathetic branches of the autonomic nervous system. A higher HRV indicates a more regulated and flexible nervous system, while a lower HRV indicates a more dysregulated and rigid nervous system.

A HRV monitor is a device that can measure your HRV using sensors attached to your chest, wrist, ear, or finger. The device can display your HRV data in real time, as well as store and analyze it over time. You can use a HRV monitor to track your vagus nerve activity and the effects of vagus nerve stimulation on your nervous system. You can also use a HRV monitor to guide your vagus nerve stimulation, by adjusting the frequency, duration, and intensity of your practices according to your HRV feedback.

There are many types of HRV monitors available on the market, with different features, functions, and prices. Some examples of HRV monitors are Polar H10, Oura Ring, Elite HRV, and Biostrap. You can choose the HRV monitor that best suits your needs and preferences, and consult the user manual or the manufacturer's website for instructions on how to use it.

How to Create a Personalized Vagus Nerve Stimulation Plan

Creating a personalized vagus nerve stimulation plan can help you achieve your goals and optimize your vagus nerve health. A vagus nerve stimulation plan is a structured and customized plan that outlines the specific practices, frequency, duration, and intensity of your vagus nerve stimulation, as well as the expected outcomes and indicators of progress. A vagus nerve stimulation plan can also include the resources, tools, and support that you need to implement your plan.

To create a personalized vagus nerve stimulation plan, you need to follow these steps:

- Assess your current state, by evaluating your level of stress, trauma, or nervous system dysregulation, as well as your strengths, weaknesses, opportunities, and threats. You can use self-assessment tools, such as questionnaires, scales, or checklists, or consult a professional, such as a doctor, therapist, or coach, to help you with this step.

- Define your goal, by specifying what you want to achieve or improve through vagus nerve stimulation, such as your health, well-being, or performance. You can use the SMART criteria, which stands for Specific, Measurable, Achievable, Relevant, and Time-bound, to help you set a clear and realistic goal.

- Choose your practices, by selecting the vagus nerve stimulation practices that appeal to you and suit your needs and preferences, such as breathing exercises, yoga, meditation, music, art, physical activity, social support, or therapy. You can use the tips and strategies for optimal vagus nerve health, as well as the information and recommendations from reliable sources, such as books, articles, podcasts, or experts, to help you with this step.

- Schedule your sessions, by deciding the frequency, duration, and intensity of your vagus nerve stimulation sessions, as well as the time and place of your sessions. You can use the guidelines and suggestions from the sources that you consulted, as well as your own experience and feedback, to help you with this step. You can also use a calendar, planner, or app to help you organize and manage your sessions.

- Monitor your progress, by measuring and tracking your vagus nerve activity and the effects of vagus nerve stimulation on your nervous system, using a HRV monitor or other tools, such as journals, logs, or charts. You can also monitor your progress by observing and recording the changes and improvements in your health, well-being, or performance, using indicators, such as symptoms, behaviors, emotions, or outcomes.

- Review and adjust your plan, by evaluating and reflecting on your progress and achievements, as well as the challenges and difficulties that you faced, using the data and feedback that you collected. You can also review and adjust your plan by celebrating and rewarding yourself for your efforts and accomplishments, as well as seeking and applying feedback and support from others, such as friends, family, or professionals.

By following these steps, you can create a personalized vagus nerve stimulation plan that can help you regulate your nervous system and enhance your health and well-being. You can also revise and update your plan as you go along, to suit your changing needs and preferences.

Conclusion

With this book, you have learned about the vagus nerve, a major nerve that connects the brain to various organs and influences our psychological and physical well-being. You have also learned about the polyvagal theory, a scientific framework that explains how the vagus nerve has evolved in three stages and three behavioral strategies: the dorsal vagal complex, the ventral vagal complex, and the smart vagus. Each branch is associated with different physiological and emotional responses to the environment and social interactions.

You have discovered how to stimulate the vagus nerve, both internally and externally, to regulate the nervous system and activate the ventral vagal complex and the social engagement system, which are responsible for emotional regulation, communication, and connection with others. By stimulating the vagus nerve, you can enhance your sense of safety, well-being, and trust, as well as improve your digestion, immunity, and healing.

You have explored the benefits and applications of vagus nerve stimulation for various aspects of your health and well-being, such as stress, trauma, anxiety, depression, inflammation, pain, immunity, digestion, heart health, brain health, and social health. You have also learned how to measure and monitor your vagus nerve activity using a device called a heart rate variability monitor, which reflects the balance between the sympathetic and parasympathetic branches of the autonomic nervous system.

You have created a personalized vagus nerve stimulation plan, by assessing your current state, defining your goal, choosing your practices, scheduling your sessions, monitoring your progress, and reviewing and adjusting your plan. You have also learned how to overcome the common pitfalls and challenges that may arise along the way, such as overstimulation, understimulation, resistance, avoidance, expectations, and comparisons.

Now that you have reached the end of this book, you have gained the knowledge and skills to incorporate vagus nerve stimulation into your daily life, and to optimize your vagus nerve health. However, this is not the end of your journey, but rather the beginning. Vagus nerve stimulation is not a one-time event, but a lifelong practice. It requires consistent effort, patience, and perseverance, as well as curiosity, openness, and flexibility.

Therefore, we encourage you to continue your vagus nerve stimulation practice, and to experiment with different methods, techniques, and tools that suit your needs and preferences. We also encourage you to share your experiences and insights with others, and to seek and offer support and feedback. Vagus nerve stimulation is not only a personal practice, but also a social practice. It can help you connect with yourself, with others, and with the world.

We hope that this book has inspired you to take charge of your nervous system, and to enhance your health and well-being. We hope that you have found vagus nerve stimulation to be a rewarding and enjoyable practice, and that you have experienced positive changes and improvements in your life. We hope that you have discovered the power and potential of your vagus nerve, and that you have unlocked the secrets of the polyvagal theory.

"Thanks for reading" I hope you found this book valuable! If you did, your feedback on Amazon would be incredibly helpful. Sharing your thoughts is a great way to support authors and connect with other readers who are interested in similar topics. Let's build a community of learning and growth. Together, we can make a positive impact!" We thank you for reading this book, and we wish you all the best in your vagus nerve stimulation journey.